Deep Ends

poems by

Roberta Schultz

Finishing Line Press
Georgetown, Kentucky

Deep Ends

Copyright © 2025 by Roberta Schultz
ISBN 979-8-88838-835-8 First Edition
All rights reserved under International and Pan-American Copyright Conventions. No part of this book may be reproduced in any manner whatsoever without written permission from the publisher, except in the case of brief quotations embodied in critical articles and reviews.

Publisher: Leah Huete de Maines
Editor: Christen Kincaid
Cover Art: Chris Arvidson, "Dear Lake Michigan"
Author Photo: Kevin Nance
Cover Design: Elizabeth Maines McCleavy

Order online: www.finishinglinepress.com
also available on amazon.com

Author inquiries and mail orders:
Finishing Line Press
PO Box 1626
Georgetown, Kentucky 40324
USA

Contents

Wade in the Water

Lesson 1
Shimmy 2
The Recipe 3
Documentation 4
Pyramids 6
Cross Chest Carry 7
Indecent Exposure 8
Sakura 9
Tlingit Drum 10
Thicker Than Blood 11
Whitewater 12
Divining 13
Triplets 15
Grief 16
End Times 17

The Water is Wide

Lanyard Diptych 23
On Learning "Mending Wall" by Heart 24
Dear Margaret Atwood 25
Interview 27
The Bean Trees in English III 28
Choreography 29
Naawakamig 30
Making Fry Bread at the New Year's Eve Sobriety Powwow 31
Ancestor Stories 33
Drum 34

One!	35
After Boots and the Princess are Married a Long Time	36
Upright	37
The Last Word	38
Gangland Legacy	39
The Target is Hardened	41
What I Mean When I Say *I'm not invisible*	42
Walking Out of Ukraine	43
The Fittest	44

By the Waters of Babylon

Deep Ends	47
Flood Prophecy at Hindman, KY	48
Change in the Flight Plan	49
For the Birds	50
The Healing Question	52
I Imagine You in Greenland	54
Live as if You are Already Dead	55
The Dead Speak as Hades Floods Over	56
The Brave Must Stay to Watch	57
My Hands Trust Love	58
Understory	59
Epoch	60
Fire Ring	61
I Heed Wendell Berry's Advice on How to Poem	62
Byzantine	63
Mockingbird	64
Unsubmittable	65
That Time of Fear Thou Mayst in Me Behold	66
In the Grass	67
Bones in the Woods	68
Yosemite	69
Poem Begun with a Line from Denton Loving	70

Wade in the Water

Lesson

Like Tarzan in leopard skin
I swam underwater, free.

Mom and Aunt Marge paddled like
dogs, their heads above surface.

To teach me how to survive,
those traitors tossed me in the

deep end. I gasp for air still.

Shimmy

Breathe in to flood all
senses with the splash
of words.

Trace torrents
through vessels
toward the heart.

Open aerobic prayers.
Bend, flex, breathe out
some shimmy to wash
the globe
with shine.

With breaking waves
of lullaby, rock
this dizzy world
to its knees.

The Recipe

We are some sad-ass bad cooks in my family.
The circle of writers shares sacred recipes
from ancestors we are here to explore.
My people left home because there was no food.

The circle of writers shares sacred recipes,
but all I call up is the back of a box.
My people left home because there was no food,
hoping the new world held fuller pantries.

But I all call up is the back of a box
of barley my mom used to make her soup.
Hoping the new world held fuller pantries,
we stirred pots over a hot plate in the back room.

Of barley my mom used to make her soup
along with scraps that lasted the week.
We stirred pots over a hot plate in the back room.
Specks of onion, chunks of celery, bits of carrot

along with scraps that lasted the week.
We added canned tomatoes and bouillon,
specks of onion, chunks of celery, bits of carrot.
Hearty vegetable barley soup supposes there is meat.

We added canned tomatoes and bouillon
so that the broth always tasted like beef at least.
(Hearty vegetable barley soup supposes there is meat.)
We are some bad-ass sad cooks in my family.

Documentation

Lined up next to the livery,
a chorus line of beer wagons

set to deliver the first Wiedemann's Fine
after Prohibition.

My grandpa, Clifford Stephens,
remembered this event as historical,

told me he delivered the first
barrel on that momentous day.

All I could call up for image
was his barrel chest,

his suspendered work pants
tugged way past his natural waist,

glasses fogged with pride when
my sister and I played "Tom Dooley" after supper,

his scraped elbows wrapped in plastic,
deepening the infection that landed him

on his back, small and silent, at Speers Hospital.
His half-German warbling *Ach de lieber*

as he poured me a juice glass
of bohemian lager.

Not one of us thought beer was anything
but nourishing liquid bread.

One day I googled *first beer
after Prohibition in Northern Kentucky*

to find black and white witness
for my grandpa's claim to fame:

4th wagon from the left, a driver in suspenders,
horses ready, gold rims sliding down his nose.

Pyramids

My dad stretches out on the floor, in corpse pose,
a thirty-inch pyramid spanning his core.
In and out, he practices cleansing breath
while I watch for something big to happen—
like a burst of light or a low cosmic hum.
He teaches a class in how to expand
to nuns at Villa Madonna College.
He hypnotizes me each night to become.

Afterwards, he still sells shoes at Thom McAn.
I do not fly from my imprinted nest
of first grade redbird readers. Even so,
Swedish tetra boxes save milk in Europe,
make food easier to ship, harder to spoil.
The Universe, as we know it, ripples on.

Cross Chest Carry

After the war, he suffered a *nervous breakdown*.
Spent some time at the State Hospital
in Louisville.

We never lit fire crackers on Fourth of July.
He allowed sparklers, but still winced
at their flare.

I never knew a father who loved noise or bustle.
He preferred skiffs to troll across glassy lakes, his back
in opposition to Grandpa's.

At night, he puzzled over *The Racing Form*, scribbled
stats from a bookie's system, practiced endless
penmanship loops on steno pads.

His quirks did not seem strange to me. I never knew
a father who didn't wear solid colors, who didn't buy
five of the same black shirt.

So that day, after Stephen's diagnosis, my sister and I sat stunned
in Newport McDonald's. In lockstep, grandpa and grandson
walked on toes toward the counter.

Heads up in the current of light and sound, they rocked—
from side-to-side to stay alert for our order.
Two lifeguards synchronized their measured crawl.

Indecent Exposure

He carries letters until he can't
remember why there are mail boxes.

Walks his route five miles a day anyway,
across the bridge and over the flood wall path.

Whistles, watches the river,
and sometimes stops by a coffee shop

just as the sun disappears over Covington.
Lingers in a bookstore before

shuffling after shadows backwards in time.
Sometimes he wanders into 1987.

Forgets that he no longer owns
the broken-down Rambler. And halfway

across the flood wall, approaches the Fourth Street bridge,
where he almost always has to pee.

He takes a leak behind a scant lamppost
when the cop appears near his elbow.

He never, ever forgets my phone number.

Sakura

Strikes on a tongue drum call me to the sound bath. The leader wields rubber mallets to shower our circle in deep gongs of pentatonic buzz. Echoes warm and stir waiting cores with breeze. Sweet blossoms of memory scatter, then fade into jangle of Japanese song for new beginnings. Notes bubble up in my throat, recall how I sat, poised to gulp sake. His swift fingers swept a too-full and tilted ochoko from my grip.

When my Japanese
penpal came to stay with us,
I learned to savor.

Tlingit Drum

The drum appears
on my mother's desk
in the Billing Department
of Palm Beach Company.

My daughter will like this,
she tells the grateful salesman
who brought this token home
from the road, a *thank you*
for Mom's special care
with numbers.

With each frame turn,
two images rotate right—
raven, whale, raven, whale—
cornflower blue, shaded black
eyes painted by hands that weave
broad hats from cedar strips.

Once in my grasp, the drum
opens doors to heartbeats,
to honor beats, to powwows,
to potlatch to hoop dance,
to grass dance and ever-
widening circles.

The people's name clicks
in my throat like new
language where raven
and whale and cedar
speak all names
in cadence.

Thicker Than Blood

My dad had the Blackfoot blood,
so I reasoned he'd value the lesson,
from my hands, it is sacred.

As a boy, he tagged after Grandpa Price,
asked all about his journey east to Ohio, all about
indentured servant papers, all about the roustabout life.

I signed him up to make native drums with me.
He nodded as our teacher went over each step—
why these drums could not contain metal.

He sang along with the AIM song. He sang along
to the vocable chant of "Amazing Grace." He laughed
at the punchline to "Gaggleshawn" when drummers from Leech Lake

explained Ojibwa words. How a brand new car might find its way
into 21st Century powwow songs. When it came time to lace up the drum
in the intricate weaving tradition, my dad let go of his rope

to the gene pool. He tumbled head-first into a deep end,
splashed and thrashed hard, kicked away from the rescue of ritual.
Drum-making was taking too much of his time.

With two days to go
in our week-long workshop,
my dad showed our teacher his shortcut—

so proud of his staple gun pattern through elk hide.
All done. He smiled. *What now?* Next workshop,
I signed up my white-from-Kentucky mother.

Whitewater

The last words we speak
gurgle over the phone
from your hospital bed.
Your husband's family
laughs casually in
riffles.

A rushed question streams from your throat,
are they coming? As he pushes the receiver
toward your hand, he assures me that you
will be home
tomorrow.

I want to hear your lips channel
plans for a next day when we
cast sister babble across
hidden boulders
into pocket
water.

Instead, bubbles rise,
ripple out to

something about mind
       the nurses.
Something about rest.
Something about wait
       for our own wake.
Something I will reel in
forever—

that I cannot fish *goodbye*
from these swollen
rapids.

Divining

You lean into loss
like a dowsing rod. Ribs slat
down toward red sand.

You sing through that ring
in your ears and shuffle feet
to follow the pulse.

Verbs scrape at scars,
peel pale layers
from dark skin.

Strange poems rattle
from wounds this deep. They skitter
wry songs like stones tossed

into a dry well.
You bend crafted lines into
folds, file them away

like taxes.

Like taxes, folds file
them away. You bend crafted
lines into a dry well.

Wry songs— like stones tossed
from wounds this deep—they skitter.
Strange poems rattle

from dark skin, peel pale
layers. Verbs scrape at scars.
To follow the pulse

in your ears and shuffle feet,
you sing through that ring
down toward red sand

like a dowsing rod.
Ribs slat. You lean
into loss.

Triplets

This wild dance   tapping code   down the dark   and narrow
dream hallways.   Manic stance   where three jams   over two

like a ghost   now muffled   forever   except in
beats pounding   out patterns   that signal   a life force

so that two   never morphs   into heart   threnody.
Always that   keeping on   even pulse   drags along

over floors   peanut shelled   in memory   of sisters.
There were three,   but now two.   I feel feet   shuffle slow.

There were three,   but now two.   I feel feet   shuffle slow
over floors   peanut shelled   in memory   of sisters.

Always that   keeping on   even pulse   drags along
so that two   never morphs   into heart   threnody

beats pounding   out patterns   that signal   a life force
like a ghost   now muffled   forever   except in

dream hallways.   Manic stance   where three jams   over two.
This wild dance   tapping code   down the dark   and narrow.

Grief

Once pain blew me up
into a swollen balloon,
I tried to avoid all
points & pricks &
sharp tongues,

but they cut
unexpected.

Like when my friend—
a songwriter
whose brother
killed himself—
warned me,

*don't say anything
depressing.*

I squealed into the ether,
then disappeared.

Maybe you saw me
on the sidewalk—
rubber busted blue.

Ribbon tail plastered
to concrete
by foot falls.

Waiting for rain
to wash away
what's left.

End Times

After our women's circle,
the church psychic moved
to the top of a hill.

She gave up reading
for birthday parties.
Told Mom to stay away
from rivers and cities.

> We were on the highest hill
> in Bellevue, sipping
> red wine after
> birthday cake.
>
> The evening's entertainment,
> a reading for each
> woman:
>
> Mom, Shirley the Organist,
> my two sisters, and me.
>
> Each of us took our solo turn
> in Shirley's downstairs den,
> seated in the high-backed
> chair, facing the seer's
> closed eyes.
>
> The rest of us finished the Pinot Noir,
> waiting our turns in the warm buzz
> of sulfites and sunset, giggling
> at what might be uncovered
> by prying second sight.

I entered the low-lit consult where
the psychic fingered a bead loop.
Pink orbs cascaded over
her blue tunic from a knot
tied under her neck.

Her eyes wide open, she began,
*There's a woman here, hovering close.
She wants you to*—she paused
to touch her own throat—*she
wants you to vocalize.*

She pronounced *vocalize* as if
the word itself choked her
with sharp syllables.

>Back upstairs in Shirley's kitchen,
>we shared some coffee, compared
>our reading notes, laughed
>at what each message might
>or might not mean.
>Mom was the last
>to descend
>the stairs.

Her reading didn't last long.
We watched as the psychic
scrambled up the stair well,
grabbed her purse to rush
through the side door
without saying goodbye.

Mom sat down at the kitchen table,
a little pale and out of breath.
What on earth did you ask her?
Shirley pushed a cup of coffee
Mom's way.

*Nothing about me. I just asked
what will become of this sad, sad world?*

I wonder about that psychic as I watch the news
years later. Does she still see fires and floods?
Or the spattered blood of children shot down?
Do the winds wail at the crest of her sentry hill—
a gale force keening from the ancestors?
If I *vocalize* these days,
will anybody hear me?

The Water is Wide

Lanyard Diptych

1. Yellow, red and orange strands of plastic braided on a metal loom. Summer at the schoolyard pool. The older girls advising us *over, under, over, under* until we could slide your knotted loop over our heads, have something we could own besides the multicolored potholders we proudly presented to smiling mothers at summer's end. The silver whistle was a nice touch, turning us all into junior lifeguards. I find you tucked inside my desk drawer.

2. Coiled like a brilliant braided snake, I find you in the keepsake chest my high school boyfriend made in shop, my nickname carved boldly onto the lid in large beveled letters. Next to my archery patches, under my hunter safety badge. I need you now. *Over, under, over, under* sing the camp swimming instructors. *Don't ever work as a lifeguard on open water*, advises my life-saving instructor after I drag a 215 lb male classmate out of the campus pool. I win my certification, feel the silver cool of your whistle dangle against my ever-bronzing chest.

On Learning "Mending Wall" by Heart

Spring breathes mischief
through my speech teacher and me.
We know my shyness

will never carry
oratory or drama.
But question, I can—

in quiet earnest
tones of wondering beyond
my father's sayings.

Some words roll and bounce
like balls, far away
from my memory's grasp.

I mend all gaps
with constant repetition—
my psalm-learning scheme.

Frozen ground swell sings,
*Something there is that doesn't
love a wall, that wants...*

elves to destroy it.
Tumble down, boundary of fear.
Fall like Jericho.

Dear Margaret Atwood

*—You fit into me
like a hook into an eye*

*a fish hook.
an open eye. (Power Politics)*

Back then when
I studied poets
they were mostly men
except, of course,
dear Auntie Em
who many liked
to write off
as spinster, but now
how hard she is
to ignore.

Back then when
I was a charter
subscriber to *Ms,*
I read about you
in *Time*, sent off
at once for your
hardback poems,
Power Politics.

Something about hook & fish—
Something about open & eye.
I knew what you meant
ten times over.

Ten years rising,
ten years struggling,
I read about Aunts
in *The Handmaid's Tale,*
thought you warned
against impossible danger—
theocracy could never
happen here.

But now how hard
you are to ignore.

Denay Nunavit, I say
while munching on
some Chickie Nobs.

Believe every bit.
Believe it.

Interview

No high school wanted to pay
a newly-minted M.A.
(with no experience)
to teach English
and coach volleyball.

But, I decided if I wore my silky new
powder blue pantsuit inspired
by "The Porter Wagoner Show,"
someone, somewhere would see
my shine.

So, I drove my '65 VW Beetle
out route 32 to Clermont County.
Told that principal of course
I could coach volleyball—
even though I'd last
played in 7th grade—
went on and on about
how I loved to write,
sprayed sass
around his office
like Aqua Net.

I could tell I would not get the gig.

Halfway home, the tie rod scraped
paint off the *do not pass* line.
I imagined Dolly driving backroads
home from a long country tour.

A sleek and can-do woman jumped out
of my car, hoisted thin rusty metal
from the road, lashed it to the axle
with her matching beaded hair tie.

I brushed dirt from my sparkly
sky blue ass, waved and blew kisses
at the farm boys whistling past
in their Ford pickup truck.

The Bean Trees in English III

Where are you from?
The immigrant restaurant workers
query my dark-skinned 11th grade student.

From here. I live right over there.
Nathan points toward Villa Hills
north, by the river.

They laugh. Confer in Spanish.
Laugh some more.
That can't be true.

*But it is. I've lived here
my whole life.*

The dishwasher translates
for the rest of the crew
on break in the back lot.

More Spanish, more laughter.

What are they laughing about?
(Nathan probably wishes he'd paid
more attention in Spanish 100.)

The dishwasher pats him on the shoulder.
*They say you cannot be from here
because you work too hard.*

The next day in American Lit,
Nathan raises his hand,
before I ask the class,

Any thoughts on chapter 10?
Then, clears his throat
to begin.

Choreography

Aunt
Em,
your verse
not quite rhyme,
your ballad beats sung
to the tune of Gilligan's Isle.
Students tap pencils on scoresheets
for Advanced Placement—
bob their heads,
dance each
line
new.

Naawakamig

> *—in the middle of the earth (Ojibwa language)*

His brown hands
working hard
at a drum.

His long hair.

His language.

His mother.

His respect for the Mother,
all mothers.

Each stolen way
left him a fool
for knowing how.

Left his shoulders slumped
like a school boy caught,
eyes wide with surprise
at every lesson.

Neck thrust ever forward
like a turtle stretches
toward sun.

Making Fry Bread at the New Year's Eve Sobriety Powwow

The line for Indian tacos snaked through concessions
and backed up toward the ticket booth.
Our emcee could see that human anaconda
from his announcer's table along the gym sidelines.

I watched him pass the microphone to the head dancer
then march toward the entrance of Holmes High School.
From my ticket booth view, I could hear apologies
from native patrons paying with Jacksons.

Mundane tally of receipts gave me an upfront
eye and ear on each *a ho* and grunt of agreement.
I could hear the fry bread crew of older women laughing
as they worked dough into tasty taco beds.

One of them spied the emcee stomping along the gym floor
toward their busy concession. She thrust out her lower lip,
threw back her head to indicate to the other women
that a famous activist from the Occupation of Wounded Knee

was headed their way in a hurry. They all continued
making and serving Indian tacos, heads down.
The emcee slipped inside the side door to their service counter.
What do you need, brother? asked the fry bread chef.

Her knuckles met her hips in fists, her shoulders thrown back
in a stance I recognized as *approach at your own peril*.
I stopped counting money. The ticket takers inhaled.
Patrons quit sliding Jacksons through the booth window.

This line is moving much too slowly, the emcee began.
*Maybe we should organize more like a mess hall. More
like an assembly line, like we did in the Air Force.* The fry bread chef
was not impressed, She pulled an apron from the door hook

tossed it at the emcee's chest. Then she held up her hands—
dusted with flour, fingers spread wide—in front of his opened eyes.
*I've been making fry bread in this hot kitchen for four hours straight.
Do you know what I—what any of these women here—could do to you*

with our strong hands? The rest of the fry bread crew looked up to smile, then went straight back to work assembling Indian tacos. I resumed counting, ticket takers exhaled, Jacksons flowed under the glass. The emcee ducked under the yoke of his apron, then washed his hands to work hard dough.

Ancestor Stories

You can't believe the history
which is largely nonexistent,
disappearing into black holes
no longer acknowledged
as real.

Oral cultures count on stories,
not called myth by those who
pass them on.

Take that question—
How long have you lived here?
Always, sing the stories.
Always, chants Vine Deloria, Jr.
Scholar, thinker, not a scientist
as such, but well-read and listened
in the stories used against.

Land bridge from Asia, say textbooks
written by people for whom that story
fits narrative.

Whose story? Theirs. His
Land bridge went two ways, right?
asks the Main Vine. *Megafauna*
don't read road signs.

So, let me tell you this…
Scientists—not even ones
from a tribal nation—found
some really old fossil footprints
on this self-same land backing
the ancestor stories.

Photoshopped! Fake News!
Boo-hoo! Hooey!
claim the usual suspect
suspects, for whom
all story is made up.

Drum

I dream that its true name pounds
in the part of my ear that is namesake,
vibrates like stretched alligator
with necessary membrane.

Framed with wood or bone or metal,
taut spirit beings were born in Asia.
Planet Drum, says Mickey Hart,
suggesting that we all pull skin

tight enough to strike
with beaters and fingers.
Mallets tap tabors, transform
tympanum with choral thunder.

Cadence triumphs over chaos.
When we mark time
as heart beat, we
begin together.

One!

cry all the *drum* derivations. You can hear echoes in Middle Dutch *tromme* or 15th Century's *drom*. *d's* and *t's* dance on tongues like Tao's ancient paradox.

Stretched alligator membrane moans the first prehistoric beats from its ghost heart. Spirit beings learn to count by songs of sacrifice. The living join in.

Skin spans the spaces over frames of wood, bone, crock, gourd, and metal. Hands strike hide with palm, finger, thumb, mallet, stick. Breach each silence with a numbered prayer.

After Boots and the Princess are Married a Long Time

—a sequel to a fairy tale from Norway

My backbone won't snap
like your fingers.
My backbone will sway
the way crowded saplings
sprout into maple
covens.

My backbone will dance
in a circle of bowed heads,
tumble leaves to ground
like Rapunzel's
golden stair.

I fancy how to cobble my backbone
from yonder sea foam, vow never
to cut a sorry figure who stumbles
and mumbles away empty
from brew vats, bound
to serve, bound
to wife.

Now that's a story—
a wife romps under
the Blood Moon, drains
her ale cup, tips the barkeep,
then whistles her way home
alone along dark paths.

There in the clearing,
her bright hovel waits,
tree lit by window,
husband at door.

Upright

Gary on the tractor. Gary at the check-out knowing
the bagger's name when I can't recall the person's
face he shows me in Sunday's obits.

Gary, young—broad in the neck and shoulders,
even wider in the places that accept. Gary talking
back to the local news when all they know is beer
fests and holiday walks when every day someone
is just trying to live under a tarp by the river.

Gary—old since 34 when a shelf fell on his head
at work and caused one side of his body to drag
behind the other, making every step he takes
a measured invocation to the gods of gravity.

Behold the hard-won balance of an upright man.

The Last Word

To place one door in front of the other sounds easy
until old sayings pack their bags. Adages slam shut,
stomp hollow tantrums on hardwood. Proverbs echo,
trail off to whimper thin trills over transoms.

At first, you follow them across thresholds, reach
for the light switch inside each entry.
You glimpse the last word disappear
behind stained walnut panels.

If a warning tremor didn't jounce your hand
like water in a tumbler, if ice crystals didn't case
your larynx, muffle volume, slow your speech,
maybe you could catch them, call them back.

Well-meaners remind: *one foot in front of the other.*
You feel locks click into place, find no key beneath the mat.

Gangland Legacy

It's been years since they moved to Las Vegas,
left a seam of gritty girlie bars along the strip,
where that leader of 500 swore
he would clean it all up,
close it all down right before
the waitress slipped him the *mickey*,
his slack face plastered above the fold
on every tabloid rag in the region.
nuzzling a half-naked stripper.

It's been decades since my dad drove past
a cottage near Pike 27 Drive-In, slowed
at the light, cued mimicked music
from *The Twilight Zone,* orated
in his best Rod Serling rasp,
That door was built from human bones.

I was 5 or 6 when my dad first took me to the bookie
which I thought was a bookstore, which was, in fact,
a store filled with paperback books where my dad
ducked away to the *back to see a man
about a horse,* which I took as code
for the bathroom.

All through the '60s, one after another, restaurants
and nightclubs burst into flame. *Suspicious fire,*
said newsman, Al Schottelkotte, *film at 11.*
The man with the scary door
jumped from his hospital
room at St. Luke's
to his death.

In the '70s, one of my husband's massive
classmates from St. Joe's left town
to work security at the Flamingo.

In the '80s, we sat at a 7th Street bar with Johnny,
sang along to his all-Sinatra jukebox,
listened to wistful stories about

Havana and *the old days.*

So last night, when the air burned familiar
with grainy smells, cameras focused
on Wilder, KY. A truck exploded,
catching an empty produce warehouse
on fire. *Someone wanted out
of the vegetable business,*
I mused, out of habit.

The Target is Hardened

You assume your prey is soft
and scared, pounding away
from shuffled sounds in the brush,
shaken by senseless side steps.

While we sigh—wily and worn—
at thoughts & prayers & platitudes,
we take aim, shoot steady

hollow point bullets
through your fallacies.
Your Kevlar chest shreds.
When will that stone
you call a heart
explode?

What I Mean When I Say *I'm Not Invisible*

after Eve L. Ewing

I mean that I see you side-eye when I walk by.
I mean that you follow my shadow out the door
and down the night street. I mean that when I slip
into an alley and wait for you to slide by on slick
pavement, you probably sniff woodsmoke curl
from rusty barrels at water's edge where
what smolders often combusts.

I mean that when you come face-to-face
with me, one homeless man in two coats
as I rattle a shopping cart
against each curb, you step
through the atomized
mist of my bones.

Walking Out of Ukraine, a Cento

Imagine that you see
the wretched strangers.
They do not weep:
their eyes are too raw for tears.

Their babies at their backs
and their poor luggage,
groundsheets and blankets spread
on the muddy ground.

Past them have hastened
processions of retreating gun teams.

And it is not for us to make them an anthem:

Once we had a country and we thought it fair.
Look in the atlas and you will find it there.

No refuge from the skirmishing fine rain,
plodding to the ports and coasts
for transportation.

No one leaves home unless
home is the mouth of a shark.

Lines selected from the following poems: "The Book of Thomas More" by William Shakespeare, "The Refugees" by Sir Herbert Read, "In October 1914 (Antwerp) by Ford Madox Ford, "Refugee Blues" by W.H. Auden, "All Day it Has Rained" by Alun Lewis, "Home" by Warsan Shire

The Fittest

> —*"Let's Go, Darwin! (a meme posted on facebook in early 2022.)*

Someone finally posted that meme—
the one urging Darwin to be right
in his theory that nature will
mete out a hard brand
of justice.

I've seen too many songbirds smashed
into mirrors of window woods
to believe such gavels
rap for just rule.

Instead, thunder pounds down so wild and hungry,
all feathers howl into spiral, swallowed
by the throat of a roaring,
soaring vortex.

By the Waters of Babylon

Deep Ends

    —Inspired by Jericho Brown's "Duplex"

He tumbles head-first into deep ends.
I call on my life-saving lessons.

    Memory stalls this uncertain lifeguard:
    more off the board, less cannonball style.

More off like a cannon shot from the bow,
heat-seeking beneath the murky surface.

    Hide-and-seek, he murks beneath green surface,
    sinks to the bottom like a blood-stained lure.

Sinkers won't lure this red and white bobber down.
This Bobby still bounces, bubbles back, this buoy.

    This boy was once my father, my namesake.
    For the sake of our names, I learn to float.

Always a floater who rises again when
he tumbles head-first into deep ends.

Flood Prophecy at Hindman, KY

A heron squawks over the big screen
at the feet of towering peaks
where writers huddle near
to hear one teacher's
words translated
into film.

His cry pierces the twilight hush— all eyes and ears
flush with struggle to rush home to their rooks
before a rolling bulge of clouds explodes
such fragile nests.

Change in the Flight Plan

There's a moment when each hard-spun
thread of your solo husk
flutters free.

You unfold to fly inside a gaudy,
yet holy, orange swarm where wings
pulse common purpose through oceans of air.

For the Birds

I tell them I will sing some songs
that are *for the birds.*

They laugh, so I tell them how I learned
that robins do not usually eat seeds.

I found out when I tried to force feed
earthworms to an injured dove.

A Raise and Release bird woman explained,
some birds eat seeds, others do not.

I'd been nursing the draft of a song
about seed eaters. I called it *The Robin Song.*
I knew nothing then. I know so little still.

At least I know how songs
might lose the taste of truth.

I share my edit with the Sisters,
insert a seed-eating bird,
keep prosody with a pleasing
number of syllables,

In *The Redbird Song, he finds the seed
to feed his need for singing.*

They listen. The sleeping nun opens
her eyes for three minutes, props
open her thin door to real.

I say I feel bad for all robins
I meant to honor. So, we sing
a standard from 1926…

no more sobbin' when he starts throbbin'.

They perch in a line on the balcony rail
as if they hear, as if they know.
I point, but they fly.

Did you see them? I ask.
Oh, yes, says the teacher nun.

*They come to every window
when a Sister passes.*

We sing *Amazing Grace.*
We sing *O, Sanctissima*
We sing *You are My Sunshine*

They hear you sing, says the walker nun
who punches in the code for my departure.

Outside the elevator, I read the posted warning:
Make sure that the door locks behind you.

But, someone has cracked one portal open.
I need only close my eyes.

The Healing Question

—In legends, the Fisher King's wounds are healed by a question.

The Fisher King finds me
at Lourdes Hall. He hides
amid the nuns on my birthday.
As I step off the elevator,

one nun seems adrift
in her lounge chair, like she
tends a trout line, watches
for bites on the glossy surface.

As I set up my guitar, she leans
forward to take an aide's arm,
to slowly shuffle frozen hips
and swollen ankles my way.

She thrusts a gift bag forward
from which I pull a chalice—
like the grail from Arthur's quest—
attached card calligraphed by hand.

At the inside brim
where coffee will rise
(or *tea*, the nuns chorus)
is another inscription—

inscrutable and true. Spelled
out in black script, *Blessed*.
White letters spill more *Blessed*
across pink wings that span

both sides of the cup's painted
Eden scene. Smiling nuns wait
for my response. Nervous, I ask,
Am I blessed or blesséd?

The Fisher King sister kicks up heels
with a joy that jostles the jon boat.
She rows ashore to dance away
on lithe thighs made new.

I Imagine You in Greenland

Well-versed in how to survive new ice,
you fished and sealed like before
on the mainland.

The seafaring horned men
tired of gray conquest, left
their scattered ruins
and sailed warmer

far-flung seas to people
easier climes and to pillage
brighter treasure.

And now, they war against their own.
No one left unlike enough
to plunder.

They level vast dwellings.
Set new fires that can't
be doused by tears

or rising seas. They poison
the world's bread. But you
just wait. Remember

the old ways. Your language.
The sacred place
you call home.

How someday, that name
again will mean just
what it says.

Live as if You are Already Dead

Already slow. No longer quick.
Already silent like stars.
Already dust. Eyes without fire.
Not just sleeping. In repose.
Under the dirt. Up in smoke.
In that great gettin'up morning.
Beyond the clouds. Particles
on the wind. Already relic.
Roadside shrine with a name.
Already wings. Already aboard
that gospel train. Already down
in the river. Already on the ferry.
No matter. Already energy again.

The Dead Speak After Hades Floods Over

—a poem inspired by the short film, Glory at Sea

It's hard these days to ferry souls here to Elysian Fields.
River, what river? Rough surge blurs all mystic gateways.
Big Easy rubble scumbles the shore. We shades, swept here
by storms, descend to underwater gardens for the gods,
for the good. Mostly, we just float. Or finger Mardi Gras beads
in our watered-down dreams. Ain't enough spirits left in old River Lethe
to drink off that edge loss leaves. Distant tubas moan through fog
as we sip laments, lean toward that wild rattle of a second line
marching in. One sailor listens for our drift

as his muse whispers epic poems in his ear. Eyes widen
with light while he spirals to the surface. We rock suspended
in his wake, witness his ascent, stare breathless at bubbles
that gush from born-again lungs. To lead abandoned hearts, he wades
through breakers. His deckhands craft ragged sails from grief's
faded prayer flags. Rubbery legs stumble, push off for a following sea.

The Brave Must Stay to Watch

> —*Hushpuppy in* Beasts of the Southern Wild

A word I've never seen stomps down boundaries
in a random search. I once told my sophomores
at Catholic school that I could never corral
all the words. The nerdiest boys circled my desk
in a pack—did I mention it was Catholic school?
To yip his disapproval, one said, *Oh, yes!*

You can know them all! We'll help!
They'd missed their rides home so often
that I no longer believed in coincidence.
There was something puppy about their need
to surround a lone teacher, nip notions at my heels
until I'd drive them on home in the Jeep.
There was something border collie about my bent
to round up stragglers still sniffing sweet trails
for knowledge, nose-deep in the smell of theory.

I've learned how winds and time scatter scent.
How hounds wander far beyond gathering.
Still, I track and wrangle my new word, *aurochs,*
24 hours after it stumbles onto my screen.
Extinct oxen stalk a little girl in an art film
while I open gates for shadow beasts
who follow me gladly out to pasture.

My Hands Trust Love

My hands trust love
      like heat everyone holds.
My hands trust love obsessed with soft
      that pillows the night against this wall.
My hands trust love like the hard blue of water,
      though star sad smile would have none here.
My hands trust love that can shade my friends
      with wish trees sweet as a whisper.
My hands trust love like my sister,
      who flowers in life and in death.
My hands trust love used to fear
      that hovers near in imaginary mist.
My hands trust love's dark dance,
      in the dust road's candlelight moon.

Understory

I walk into the canopy of darkness,
so lush this year with record rain.
At first, contrast clouds my lens,
so slow these days to open for low light.

But once my aperture reckons,
a silver glaze glistens on every leaf,
Catchlight puddles up from the path,
diffused by humid mist.

And here, I thought, *is how
we capture epochs, one
incremental focus at a time.*

Epoch

Chlorophyll morning.
Canopy shadow understories
paths with leaves.

Oxygen levels
swoon my dizzy breath
to prehistoric.

Rounding the trail home,
I imagine dinosaurs
trumpeting at sloths—

would not be surprised
if a pterodactyl flapped
from the heron's roost.

This is what we feared
when Godzilla smashed airplanes.
Only on reel, not for real.

Fire Ring

A damsel fly lands on a shard of limestone,
on a surface encrusted with sea creatures.

I stand at the far end of a ghost lake
where my husband has circled this pit

in a ring of fossil-embossed stones
for burning up the wild grape vines

and honeysuckle brush that rampage
and tangle the edge of the woods.

This is the ninth day of record rainfall.

Maybe the damsel fly hovers near
where an inland sea might reappear?

I Heed Wendell Berry's Advice About How to Poem

Into the wind at water's edge,
exhale each breath through silence.

Along the path of scattered leaves,
chart new maps for silence.

Over the whine of faraway roads,
hum harmonies with silence.

Under the crest of white caps,
plunge deep inside blue silence.

Against all gusts that sputter alarm,
lean into shelter of silence.

Onto pages my little words string,
bead patterned prayers to silence.

Byzantine

How twisted was your path
to me— unnoticed in sandy
curve of sun-bleached conch
for years?

Had I plucked that shell
from first-time seaside
stroll along Daytona?

Had I treasured it like booty
from the pirate ships swirled
into Outer Banks'
deceptive calm

only to forget my loot
once safe back home?

As I pull sport socks
from a suitcase side pocket,
you spill onto the white bedspread
in my conference hotel room along
with dislodged shards
of wampum.

A frontal icon of Christ worn
featureless by salt and waves.
A cross and ancient letters
on the flip side.

How did you spiral toward this
faraway world?

Lost coin with value beyond market,
you purchase such coiling story
from the throat of fate.

Mockingbird

—After "Sanctuary" by Ada Limón

Suppose it's easy for me to fly
        from one redbud limb
to the top of the United Dairy Farmers sign

and sing there in every dialect I've heard
        just once like I tried with that song "Sukiyaki"—
mimicking the sounds, but this time

chirping syllables all so right
        even birds from Japan would pause
mid-flight to bob respect.

You watch me from that liminal
        perch, wait for a tune
worth telling back,

flick your bright lined tail
        in a final salute
as you spin off riffing whirs and clicks.

I drive from the gas station
        twice-filled to whistle my
shrill notes—

and I'll be changed, changed
        from this creature,
Lord, that I am.

Unsubmittable

It is not time to press *send*.
It is time to breathe back
every green-glow
word I've tapped
into inky
night.

Every red message.
Every yellow yarn.
Every blue note
bellowed over
12 bar
pulse.

Lightning bugs glimmer
dim codes that spill
into pillows of
lake dam
clay.

Wink out *goodnight*.
Wink *out*.
Wink.

That Time of Fear Thou Mayst in Me Behold

> *—a slight rewording of Shakespeare's first line from* Sonnet 73

Blue roils foam to white
that might as well be gravity.

Filmy threads finger through soil,
reach for neighbor's loosening grip.

Waves tug at severed roots. Relentless
combs unbraid life's symbiotic tangle.

The fallen stretch bare limbs
toward kin across the swollen gulf.

Yet, skeletal soldiers brace
for a last stand. They shake

scant leaves like yellow flags.
Into the breach lean callow copses.

Arrayed in gold, they wade—mark time
behind one gray and ancient snag.

In the Grass

You coil me onto your gruesome flags.
        I rise from the rings, fangs ready.

                You blame me for your worst desires.
I loop red fruit so she might bite into ripe shine.

        Still, you curl me around the healing staff.
                There, I remind you to do no harm.

Here in the grass, my ribs tickle
        from the sizzle of each thin blade.

                My tongue flicks morning air
for honeysuckle sweetness.

        And you become that smell I slink away from—
                that dank and pungent stench of fear.

Bones in the Woods

Lately, all the bones are showing.
Like a dog who won't let go,
they gnaw at me.

Sockets haunt the mirror where
eyes should steal focus. I notice
how my pup's tiny rib niggles
at my flesh. Her jaw unhinges
as she sleeps near my knee.

It is time to build new femurs,
beg hard mandibles. Poets find anatomy
in real estate's myth, bubble and brew
a healing broth from plaster cracks.

I cease my need to pick these tibias
strewn across the trail. The baby buck
born in tall grass is now that skull cradled
in the crook of a granny grapevine's ulna.

The clavicles and pelvises I visit
line this pilgrim path.
I pass the roadside shrines
of sacred vertebrae.
All scapula and metatarsal
mobiles I design will jangle free
to chime their powdered shine
in sand and shadow.

Yosemite

I didn't believe it was real—
those falls cascading between peaks.
My mind kept telling me
I was facing a painting.

Go there and see before it burns away.
Let yourself marvel at a twelve-foot wall
of wine jugs, a pyramid erected to celebrate
some Danish rock climbers' conquest
of El Capitán.

Remember how you posed next to a tree
wider than your house.
Recall how Japanese children
clambered over rocks
in the middle of the Merced.
Appreciate the rugged hiking boots
that kept you sturdy on the rocky trail.

Have you watched the news lately?
Trees older than this country
may fall to the fire.

How will we ever learn their songs?

Poem Begun with a Line from Denton Loving

Sleep is another kind of prayer
        where minutes blur well-loved faces
into slick beads. My thumb rubs rosaries
        strung across hours of night.
To visit this sacred chapel of dark,
        untie every knotted tendon,
unlock every muscle set tight into snare,
        glide over ripples of Lethe
in an unmoored skiff, forget
        soft litanies. Sip stillness.

Acknowledgments for *Deep Ends*

The opening poem, "Lesson," first appeared in *Songs from the Shaper's Harp*, 2017, Finishing Line Press,

"The Recipe" was published under the title "We are Some Sad-ass Bad Cooks in My Family" in *Persimmon Tree's* "Poetry of the Central States," December, 2022.

"I Imagine You in Greenland" also appeared in *Persimmon Tree's* Short Take feature section, Spring, 2023.

"Cross Chest Carry" first appeared in *Panoplyzine, Issue 19* and also appears in the chapbook *Asking Price*, Workhorse Writers, April 2023.

"Indecent Exposure" appears in the chapbook, *Asking Price*, 2023.

"Tlingit Drum" appears in the 2023 anthology, *Kakalak,* Moonshine Review Press.

"My Hands Trust Love" appears in *Shotglass Journal*, issue 39.

"The Dead Speak After Hades Floods Over" and "The Brave Must Stay to Watch" both appear in the chapbook, *Asking Price*, 2023.

"The Dead Speak After Hades Floods Over" first appeared in the Blood Moon issue of *Black Moon Magazine*, Fall 2021.

"Thicker Than Blood" was published in *Stone Poetry Quarterly*, May 2022.

"White Water" and "Divining" are curated in *Of Rust and Glass, No. 11* "Scars," January 2023.

"Grief," "The Target is Hardened," "Live as if You are Already Dead," "Understory," and "Epoch" all first appeared on the LexPoMo site for Lexington Poetry Month, 2022. "Live as if You are Already Dead" was selected for the 2022 LexPoMo anthology.

"Interview" appears in *Let Me Say This (A Dolly Parton Poetry Anthology)*, Madville Publishing, 2023.

"The Bean Trees in English III" appears in *Anthology of Appalachian Writers*, Barbara Kingsolver, Volume XV Shepherd University Center for Appalachian Studies, 2023.

"Making Fry Bread at the New Year's Eve Sobriety Powwow" first appeared in *Last Leaves*, "Ancestors," Issue 4, Spring 2022.

"The Last Word" was included in *Pegasus,* Spring 2022.

"Choreography" is published in *The Fib Review,* #45, June 2023.

"The Fittest," "Change in the Flight Plan," and "Fire Ring" appear in *Anthropocene*, Studio Kroner, 2022

"Deep Ends" appears in *Kakalak 2022,* Moonshine Review Press.

"I Heed Wendell Berry's Advice on How to Poem" and "Unsubmittable" appear on *Verse-Virtual,* May 2023.

"Mockingbird" is published in Volume 26 of *Pine Mountain Sand & Gravel,* 2023.

"That Time of Fear Thou Mayst in Me Behold" was displayed at *Charlotte Art League Ekphrastic Exhibit,* March 2023 next to the painting that inspired it.

"Bones in the Woods" appears in *Pine Mountain Sand & Gravel, Vol 25,* "Appalachia: (Un) Masked, 2022.

"Yosemite" is included in *Panoplyzine,* Issue 22, September 2022

"Triplets" appeared in the debut issue of *Untelling,* the literary and art publication of Hindman Settlement School, 2024.

The author wishes to thank Kentucky Foundation for Women and Loretto MotherHouse in Nerinx, KY for providing the time and space to build this collection. She would also like to thank Katerina Stoykova for her online workshops in arranging and editing poetry collections.

Deep Ends is **Roberta Schultz**'s sixth collection of poetry. Three of her chapbooks were published by Finishing Line Press while her latest chapbook, *Asking Price*, was chosen by Workhorse Writers for their 2022 series. *Underscore*, her first full-length collection, was published by Dos Madres Press in 2022. Both song writer and poet, Schultz's work appears in
Women Speak, Vol.7 and 8, Persimmon Tree, Sheila-Na-Gig, Panoplyzine, Riparian, Pine Mountain Sand & Gravel, Kakalak, Let Me Say This (a poetry anthology with Dolly Parton as the main theme) and other anthologies. She leads drum circles and serves as an Arts in Healing musician.

For ten years, she wrote book reviews for a program called *Around Cincinnati* which aired on her local NPR affiliate, WVXU, hosted by producer, Lee Hay. She performs regionally with the all-women vocal trio, Raison D'Etre. You can find out more about her at robertaschultz.com and raison3.com .

www.ingramcontent.com/pod-product-compliance
Lightning Source LLC
Chambersburg PA
CBHW020340170426
43200CB00006B/443